Gradient

Gradient

Poems by

Ruhani

Cover image by Ariana Dideban
Cover design by Peter Selgin and Shay Culligan

ISBN: 978-1-63980-465-8

Kelsay Books
502 South 1040 East, A-119
American Fork, Utah 84003
Kelsaybooks.com

To my cousin Varun—
you are with me in every footstep.

Acknowledgments

A grateful thanks to the editors of *First Literary Review-East* for accepting for publication several of the poems that appear in this collection. I would like to thank Lisa B. Freedman and Cindy Hochman for their guidance in preparing this book for publication. Thank you to my dear friend, Ariana Dideban, for her beautiful and thoughtful book cover illustration; thank you to Peter Selgin for his vision in cover design. A warm thank you to Mimma Verduci, Duccio Trassinelli, and the artists-in-residence who influenced my work and stay at La Macina di San Cresci; thank you to Xiao Yue Shan, an inspiring poet and friend. A grateful thank you to my teacher, Ashley Warren, and professor, Steve Granelli, for believing in me. I am also thankful for my chosen family: Chandni Singhvi, Sabrina Pichamuthu, Rachel Hua, Anu Kandasamy, Ellen Park, Krishna Vedanth Eleti, Navin Sirihorachai, Catherine Cremens; and thank you to my best friend, Nisha Shenoy. Thank you to my cousin and sister, Aalana Gupta-Kaistha. Thank you to my mom, Shefalika Gandhi, for teaching me the power of devotion. I am thankful to my dad, Somesh Nigam, for his wisdom. And thank you to my brother, Vishan Nigam, for showing me the balance between ambition and selflessness.

Contents

I call you mine
the way someone saw the sunrise
and gave it a name

Renfield Drive

On Renfield Drive the sign is crooked
but the children are flat and asleep.
There are fireflies kissing streetlamps
humming an electric buzz.
The commotion plays with light
and makes the street blink.
In the middle of the night
we are still alive,
a street that breathes.
My eyes are covered
with dreams of growing up.

I blink and I'm 23.
My memory insomnia
still wanders the sleeping street.

My Best-Kept Secret

Out of everyone who admires my friend's eyes
nobody sees through to them like the sun

So deeply
she can't help but squint

So thoroughly
long after the sun has set
a ring of gold remains in the blue

So generously
I stay with the sunset a little longer

High School

Always together
we snuck out to the beach
in the middle of the night

Parking the car
impatiently running into the darkness
hoping it was the direction of the sea
Fearless

A simple conversation began
between the crashing waves
and our shaky laughter
as our footsteps struck the coast

until we finally felt the water with our toes
and huddled together until sunrise
upon which I saw their faces
for the first time in six hours

I had missed them.

As I watched their rosy cheeks
and sleepy eyes
melt into the sun
I knew that these times would become
grains of sand I'd never be able to shake
from my clothes.

Until I Realized It Was Love

A middle-school friend and I
wrote letters and passed them
to each other in the hall
to read during the next period
I never knew what that was about
until I realized it was love, and

my high school friends and I
had sleepovers
wearing big T-shirts and thongs
When all I could look at was their lips
moving slow like molasses
rewriting the script of the world
I never knew what that was about
until I realized it was love, and

a college friend and I
scratched each other's backs
When we were stressed
I'd trace her name
then she'd ask me to trace mine
She said it felt better
I never knew what that was about
until I realized it was love

Braids

Shelly,

We spent a lot of time walking through Florence
and a lot of time with each other.
The duomo loomed, listening in on confessions.
Each time we thought our conversation private,
a nearby table would quiet down
and listen to what we had to say.

I think it's because they weren't expecting
to pay attention to us, beyond
the not-so-subtle glances
at our curves in different places.

Because what they began to see,
mouths slightly ajar, were our bending
curiosities for each other. How they twisted
until they formed a braid.
I wonder, if we had known each other as children
instead of meeting in our 20s, whether we would have
sat criss-cross applesauce and given each other braids

and giggled about boys. I wonder if the man
pretending not to listen to us speaking realized
his braided cruller missed his face in an attempt
to understand intellect and femininity
sipping from the same glass.

Love,
Ruhani

Basil

Basil,
Esteemed *Basilikon phuton*
plant of kings and queens
I have grown all this way to tell you that
I, too, become more powerful when crushed

The Woman Leaving Work

In a trance on
the subway, crushed
between two men, her
fingers grazed her throat
Soothing it perhaps from
having to shout or
hiding the forming lump from
not speaking at all

Spring Has Sprung

Together, women leap without leaving their seats
then they speak without moving their lips
When we don't have the floor, we sprout from the ground
and suddenly we are there. Filling the fields

Then flower to flower, bees flying
trying to justify how we broke soil in sync
without even a touch. Stunned, they pollinate
refusing a world in which we don't kiss.

Reign

The lions hold a palace in the sky—
They roar thunder, shake manes dry
In the palace lies a fine line,
thin as hair, between fear and pride

These royal lions sound the same
in the face of danger or prey
This ancient cycle of glory and shame
What strikes from the sky isn't theirs to claim

I wish to train my lion untamed
to learn one roar despite the game
Scared or brave, I wish for the grace
To roar in a drought, roar if I reign.

Before Mirrors

Our ancestors had difficulty knowing what they looked like.
They'd brave jungles, deserts, before facing a reflection.

First thing in the morning, we look at ourselves. I have a feeling
this isn't natural.

Are we also not meant to first, feel
our thumping hearts before tending to our looks? There must
be a reason you can barely see the pulse that shakes me.

So, I have an option so early on this judgmental morning.
I've been seeking this mirror for the truth,
but it is only a frame.
If I turned it around would my vision switch too?

Or better yet—Could this mirror be two-way glass? Is there a me
on the other side, begging me to feel this treasure of a racing heart,
before racing to insult my chest?

What's New?

Hey, what's new?

Well,

The blue jay outside my window flew away and the clouds, after days, revealed the blue. The shadow of my building shifted as morning brought sundials to life. My neck was sore but not anymore. My favorites restocked at the grocery store. The pavement dried from yesterday's rain. Three Deltas traversed my windowpane. A money-plant leaf fell. Avocados ripened, but too early to tell. And Taco Bell brought the pizzas back and even the— wait, I'm losing track.

I say what I have to. I lie.

Nothing much really, what about you?

If loving you means losing direction,
I'll crumple the map without question.

Alchemy Controlled

An alchemist
stuck in bed
brown eyes
trapped
behind eyelids of lead
Willing them open
with a sun to behold
only a start
but she turned them to gold

The Mirage

I submit to the shifting sand
Chasing you is wearing me down
so I pretend this barren land
where I rest was once the bend of a river
or will one day become a lake
That you loved me once
or you will someday

The Boy & the Cloud

His fingers ran across the page out of habit
In the average cloud . . .
there is the same mass of water as 90 adult African elephants.
They're still strong.

Too young to like girls yet
he would rest on the grass
and have a romance with the clouds
wanting to lie down on them instead
Then he learned in class that he'd fall right through. Straight
to the library.

A tear began to form
but its life was short-lived
invalidated
too quickly wiped away
And just like that he found
power in the fragility
of a cloud, but refused
to see the power in his own.

How It Lasted

How it lasted:
Loving you fruitless
did not mean
I had no spine

There was no shame
in standing tall
in love that was
completely mine

Aristotle Spoke of Friendship & Dance

It's like a dance
two bruised souls inching back and forth

Then calculated sermons turn spontaneous song
to laughter untamed, tripping over ourselves unashamed

And though you are new to me
this is ancient
this moving through the world with someone else

Patience

It's noon.
If we stay here and hold still
the sun will set and
our shadows will stretch and
I've never seen where a shadow stops stretching
but I know it has to exist

Eventually we will touch the edge of this earth
but right now, we stand together at noon.

And how can you sit there and tell me
that *love* is a thing of the past
when I just mentioned the word
and you summoned faces so easily?

A Lesson on You

Varun, I'm dozing off
Maybe I should be paying attention
Science was always more your thing
The only interesting thing they've said
is that nothing can be created or destroyed
Wait a minute
could that be true?

Are you still walking this earth with me?

Look Around

Everyone is given a limited amount of words
To those who save theirs to oppress:
I ask you to look beyond
the imminent *White* clouds
You too were sculpted from space
and will yield to the soil
You too were conceived from the *Black*
and will be stilled to the *Brown*

Shoulders

My mother chanted "Stand Up Straight"
tapped between my shoulder blades
Tapping turned to record-scratching
Up, back, down. Up, back, down . . .

I thought this view so outdated
fixing posture fixes all, but
broken records still play songs
What is old is what endures

Thank you, wisdom, thank you, Ma,
for repetition, for repetition
When I was the broken one—
I dusted off your old-school tune.

My Parents Drinking Chai

After every argument
chai was served
steam released
jaws unclenched
to take the first sip

Maybe there was no question
that even regretful tongues
deserve the warmth
of a second chance or perhaps
the wear and tear of the mugs
held the chipped American
dream they still shared

I wonder if they know what this taught me:
that every sip I take is a chance
to swallow the pit in my throat
and begin again

That if I close my eyes
I can see the chai-walla
on the street corner
molding cups from clay
then folding them back
into the earth to be made afresh
knowing that he will crush
his worst creations
the same as his best

I wonder if they know what they taught me:
that we are not promised this sweetness
and these bitters to last,
something far better—
we are promised the chipped rim
of a simmering tomorrow.

Nana Papa

As a boy
he memorized the dictionary
by candlelight
One night
He blew out the candle, fell into sleep
and when he awoke
his home was no longer his
Grabbing the book
he learned to pronounce a new word
Partition (pɑɚ'tɪʃən) *n.*

Lines were drawn
and so he tried to find home
walking a tightrope
between *nostalgia* and *grit*
between bowing to *India* or praying towards *London*
between believing in *molecules* or what the *pious* men said

I continued his search.
I learned that he *was* home.
He was a pillar of memory and dreams,
and so am I,
and we had been *home* (həʊm) *n.* the whole time.

She was about as simple
as a clock holding time

Coffee with Pain & Joy

I had coffee with Pain
to whom I told:
this will pass
Pain became quiet
humbled that when the café door shut
behind her, she would already be forgotten

I had coffee with Joy
to whom I told:
this will pass
so Joy spoke louder, rushed for time
I didn't realize she had so much to say
and I let her shout until she had to leave

Sitting with Nani

Sitting by your bedside
I wish I could have seen you when
you were young and your hair flowed as black
as typewriter ink

And when you look back at me now
my roots growing gray at the age of 21
I wonder if you're thinking *What a nice surprise;*
I did not expect to see her age.

Time at the Funeral

A hazy figure
emerged behind the cremation fire
I pushed through the heavy air to meet her

It was Time
her face relaxed
with the knowledge of yesterday and tomorrow

We embraced as she whispered
It will be okay. It will be okay.

Their Chatter

I can hear their bangles clinking as my mom oils my hair
the ones whose faces I take after
I hear their chatter in my own voice
though I wish it were theirs.
They've been silenced enough.

So, one reminded me to sit still for my mom as she
worked the oil from scalp to ends and
to massage my own feet when someone steps on my toes.

One insisted I never put books on the floor.
She wants me to learn of both sundial and
clock and to question the truth and
to never let dust settle on the mind.

Another told me to receive a blessing by
holding my hand to its flame.
cover my eyes. Feel the warmth enter my temples
but not to linger. There are others waiting their turn.

And the last one told me to love others how she could not.
To offer them sweets when they insist they aren't hungry
If their eyes are aflame, to pretend I haven't heard the story before
To give air to her unbreathed affection.

Some are too quick to shed themselves
of what our ancestors knew
Shall I drape myself in the ancient?
Who knows more about life:
the living or the dead?

Sinking or Grounding

Each step we take
weighed down
quicksand
The longer we dwell
the more we don't understand
So we keep moving
ignoring the condescending stars

The Aging Sun

The sun is an adult
When she says sleep
most of us sleep
while the rebels
night shifters, fireflies
walk against
what she has made

The sun was a teen once
the deepest of sleepers
not a fan of rude awakenings
dreaming of defining the day
on her own terms

She was even a child once
In her palms we laid
hands making fists in slumber
until fingers unfurled
released us to play

Hard to argue
that she couldn't set the sky aflame
at any stage.

Boston Opens in the Dark

Feeling disoriented, I go to the theater. Lights dim.
Eyes settle into darkness.

Opening credits—an orchestra of sparrows setting
the scene. The villain enters:
A garbage truck roaring (reeking), crawling up the avenue
about to overpower, until
a train
en route to South Station
chops through the air arriving from New York
carrying the aroma of pizza-by-the-slice
saving the day, delivered to my home
by a drive-by beat of reggaeton
that's already gone, but passed the baton
back to the sparrows, flying to Fenway
announcing the win, duetting with
the crisp howling wind.

All the while I wore a half-smile
eyes now open
I end meditation
and hear the chirps,
trains, tunes
file
out
of focus.

Facing East

The sun had not appeared for days. You waited so long; you became a statue. The grass below you gave up, but the weeds embraced your ankles. You thought they were trying to swallow you into the field. You didn't care that the clouds never seemed to part. But then you realized they may have been urging you to look down, not up. You failed to notice that for many cloudy days, as your will grew stiff, the sunflowers had not been standing still. They began the day facing east, as you had been. But they continued to move as if the sun were alive, east to west, then back east for the morning. All the while flicking dew onto each other, dancing in the rain they made.

Only the oldest sunflowers stood as still as you did. Had they given up? You didn't know. All you knew was that to be a statue was a privilege you had not earned yet—not when you were shown there is more to hope than waiting for the light. Not when you have yet to try stretching your neck in search of an absent sun.

Altitude

Go to the top of a mountain
and your breath will struggle
Some air is not right for you
Turn your back on that which makes your chest tight
places
people
not meant for you
This is how I've made my peace
We will never again be in the same room
Never enough air to sustain us both

Gold

I've lived moments where something shifted
I don't know who put them here, but I'll call her Gold

I don't know what you are, but I have an idea—
You are the sun setting between New York City avenues
and the willingness of the busy to marvel
no matter how often they tell themselves to keep walking

You are the youth of an old man, when he spoke
of the first piano he ever saw: his grandmother's
He was tired, this grandson
He rubbed his eyes with the back of his hands
Gold, I don't know what you are
but you could be the youth of an old man

And what else could you be aside from all that I have seen,
all that I am never meant to see?
Gold, you are the loves I never had
you're the one who put them in my head

But you're also the turn of my neck
toward what I have
and my promised youth
and the sun shining down 39th.

About the Author

Ruhani was born in New York and grew up in Princeton, New Jersey. Raised as a first-generation American by Indian parents, she was surrounded by poetry. Her name, *Ruhani,* means "spiritual" in Urdu; she was given the name because her grandfather would repeat the word in his own poetry. She began to write poems, short stories, and essays at the age of eight, and followed her passion for writing to Northeastern University, where she earned a bachelor's degree in Communication Studies.

After graduating, Ruhani developed her works in *Gradient* as an artist in residency at La Macina di San Cresci. She then moved to Dublin, Ireland where she jumpstarted her career in marketing and prepared *Gradient* for publication. Now living in Brooklyn, New York, Ruhani works in advertising for the New York Public Library. Her poems were published in *First Literary Review-East* in 2023. *Gradient* is Ruhani's first book of poetry.

www.ingramcontent.com/pod-product-compliance
Lightning Source LLC
Chambersburg PA
CBHW030814090426
42737CB00010B/1271